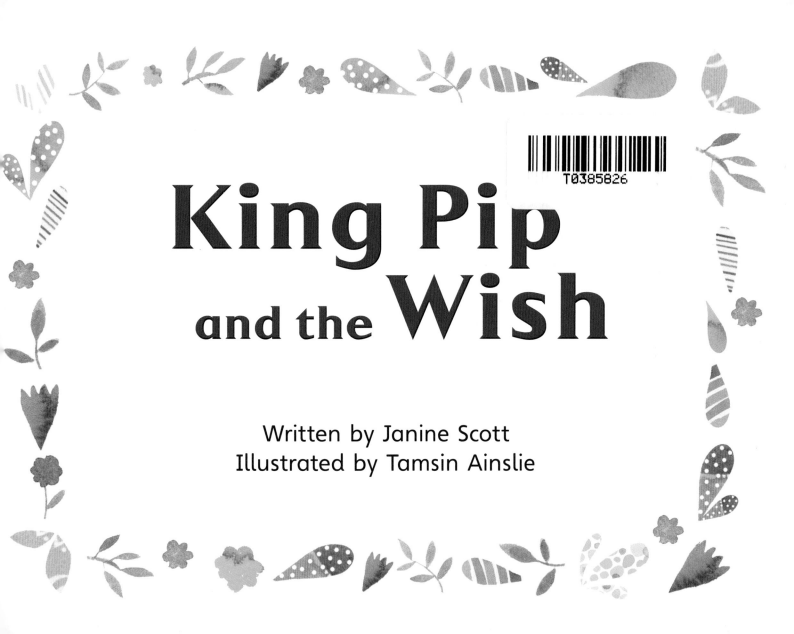

King Pip and the Wish

Written by Janine Scott
Illustrated by Tamsin Ainslie

King Pip was at a wishing well.

"I wish I had a pal," said King Pip.

WISHING WELL

3

"Will the troll be my pal?"

"No, he is no fun."

5

"Will the dragon be my pal?"

"No, she huffs and puffs."

"Will the monster be my pal?"

"No, he is too big."

q

"I wish I had a pal,"
said the monster.

"The monster wants a pal, too!"
said King Pip.

11

"You are not too big!" said King Pip.
"We can be pals."